Race and Privilege in Europe

Contents

4   Introduction

7   Quaker concern

10   Equality

10   What is race and where did come from?
12   Colourblindness
14   Racism
19   White privilege
24   Socialisation

26   Unpalatable truths

26   The invention of race
27   Missing histories: slavery and race
33   Colonial propaganda and Afrophobia today
35   Missing histories: Islam in Europe
38   Race and belonging in Europe today
41   Exclusion policy today
46   Groups openly committed to racism

51   Our place in community

52   White role to support, not lead
55   White church
67   Justice

71   Appendices
84   References and notes

Racism is a problem.

We are part of racism.

Racism can be resisted.

Race is a particularly difficult topic to talk about, especially briefly. This booklet has been written to help white people educate ourselves about racism.[i]

- Race isn't biological, it's social.
- Science tells us we're all one species, homo sapiens.
- Race is something made up, invented more recently than many people think.

Racism is part of how we have built society, part of how political, social and economic relationships are maintained.

Racism is also a powerful word. To describe something, or someone, as racist is socially significant. But what if we are part of a system which is racist, with different outcomes for people based on race? What if institutions, traditions and memories that we love reinforce and recreate racism?

---

i. This booklet uses 'we' to refer to white people. It is written for an audience that plays the dominant role in systems of racism, but has poor consciousness of the reality.

These are difficult questions to hear. Typical reactions include defensiveness and avoidance.

- *"Why focus on race? Let's think about diversity in general."*
- *"This is just who we are. Our doors are open to all, but others aren't interested in what we do."*
- *"Racism has always existed. Nothing can be done."*

The structures of racism can be difficult for white people to see. White people may also assume that racism is a problem for people of colour to address. Many of us who otherwise seek social justice do not realise how our lives reinforce racism, or what can be done to reduce it.

Reading this booklet might be an early step in seeing racism afresh, and better understanding the relationship between race and privilege. However uncomfortable, an understanding of racism is necessary for any who seek community, justice and equality.

Introduction

The Quaker Council for European Affairs (QCEA) brings a Quaker vision of peace, justice and equality to Europe and its institutions. We have been experiencing a growing awareness of racial injustice as an aspect of many of the concerns brought to us by our supporters, many of whom are members of the Religious Society of Friends (Quakers).

The human rights of migrants are a long standing concern for Quakers in Europe. QCEA has worked on issues of migration since it was founded in 1979, and undertook some particularly impactful work on racism in the 1990s.[1]

In recent years, immigration detention, racial profiling, hate crime and police violence have all been having an acute impact upon people arriving in Europe, and are harming people of colour in Europe more generally.

The racially charged stories of us and them that dominate European politics have intensified. Since the political crisis of 2015, reducing inward migration has become a central objective of European countries, and therefore of the European Union. Race has been important in the public discussion of the UK' departure from the EU, but claims of a shocking new xenophobia in Britain since the referendum ignore the long-standing experience of people of colour who research shows were on average far less surprised by the result.[2]

Racial injustice is at the root of many of the world's other most pressing issues. Military violence is primarily used against black and brown people to privilege the wealthiest (predominantly white) people. Two centuries of fossil fuel burning in the global north has caused climate change, but it is people in the global south that will be most catastrophically affected.

The story of race is also a story about us. It is not a new story, but one about a European imperial past that has been covered up and a racially stratified European experience with which the privileged group is rarely confronted.

Race can be a difficult issue to talk about

The language used to describe race changes with time and place, and many of us fear using socially inappropriate or offensive language. This book mainly uses 'people of colour', noting the increasing use of this traditionally US term in Europe too. The term sits alongside more specific identities such as black and Asian. 'People of colour' was chosen and adopted by the groups that it seeks to describe, unlike 'coloured people' which is a term created by white people during colonialism.

This book hopes to help move our understanding of race beyond language. As Quaker Rosemary Crawley has said, "Focusing too much on language enables people to reduce or conflate racism with the use of offensive language".

Origins of this book

This book was originally written in Spring 2017 to be shared informally amongst different Quaker groups in Europe. Following many requests we provide an extended and updated second edition. It has been primarily written by and for white people living in Europe, and frequently uses 'We' to address this audience.

Whilst this book focuses on race, our human experience and the privilege people are afforded in society varies widely and is affected by other forms of prejudice, discrimination and oppression, related to gender, class, neuro-diversity, sexuality and much more.

Within the context of Quaker work in Europe, this book represents an attempt to acknowledge racism, with the journey of unlearning and resisting racism still very much ahead of us. The book begins with the statements agreed by Quaker gatherings that most directly led to this work.

Andrew Lane
QCEA Director
July 2017, updated May 2019

"Non-violent living requires the unravelling of one's relationship to privilege and oppression."

— Shelly Tochluk

Responding to Quaker concern about racism: recent Quaker statements

Whether you are reading with knowledge and interest of Quakers, or not, this section records some of the statements or 'minutes' about racism agreed at European Quaker meetings.

European Quaker Statement

The 2017 Annual Meeting of the European and Middle East Section of the Friends World Committee for Consultation considered a Quaker Response to Conference of European Churches' *Open Letter on the Future of Europe*. The response was endorsed, and was commended to Quaker national structures, known as Yearly Meetings, across Europe for their own consideration. It was also taken to the Conference of European Churches General Assembly in Serbia in May 2018. An excerpt reads:

"We also believe that there needs to be a much more explicit reference to the Churches' historical complicity in, and contemporary tendency to foster, nationalism ... We need acknowledgement, repentance, and a commitment not to repeat the errors of the past, by, for instance, allowing

Anti-Semitism, Islamophobia, xenophobia and racism to go unchallenged in our day."

Quakers in Britain

Quakers in Britain made a statement on 4 February 2017, through their representative body, Meeting for Sufferings, including the excerpt:

"We condemn all acts of government which set people against one another; which discriminate against people because of who they are or where they were born. We reject policies which condone suspicion and hatred; which turn away those who need and depend upon our help. We were not put on Earth for this, but to be a people of God, to live in harmony with each other ... We stand with those whose lives are blighted by racist, discriminatory policies and those whose faith is denigrated by association with a tiny violent minority. We pray for the courage and steadfastness that will be needed as we uphold our testimony of equality, justice, peace, sustainability and truth." [i]

Quakerism does not claim to have all the answers. However, Quakers have developed questions which many people who attend Quaker Meetings find helpful to reflect upon. These two paragraphs are taken from the *Advices & Queries* of Quakers in Britain:

---

i. In reviewing the draft of this booklet, a Quaker of colour expressed disappointment that this Minute was not more self-reflective.

32. Are you alert to practices here and throughout the world which discriminate against people on the basis of who or what they are or because of their beliefs? Bear witness to the humanity of all people, including those who break society's conventions or its laws. Try to discern new growing points in social and economic life. Seek to understand the causes of injustice, social unrest and fear. Are you working to bring about a just and compassionate society which allows everyone to develop their capacities and fosters the desire to serve?

33. Bring into God's light those emotions, attitudes and prejudices in yourself which lie at the root of destructive conflict, acknowledging your need for forgiveness and grace. In what ways are you involved in the work of reconciliation between individuals, groups and nations?

"Some inequalities have become normal – we've adapted to them, making them hard to see."

— Owning Power and Privilege: Toolkit for Action, Quakers in Britain 2018

Equality

What is race and where did it come from?

Race is a type of social categorisation based on perceptions of ethnicity, and sometimes other factors such as religion, culture, nationality or legal status. More precisely race is a powerful untruth. Human racial distinctiveness is scientifically and naturally untrue. The lie says "superficial adaptations to geography (skin tone, eye shape) are genetic and biological determinants that result in significant differences among human beings".[3] As Robin DiAngelo explains in her book 'What Does it Mean to be White?', humans are among the most genetically similar species on Earth. Moreover, external appearance is not a significant indicator of difference, our individual genetics have just as much in common with people who look similar as they do with people who look different.[4]

However, it is a false concept given profound social meaning.

Social, economic and other privilege based on distinctions of religion and social status have a much longer history than racial distinctions. Differences in skin colour became a useful tool for subjugation when they were used to teach people to believe in an untruth as a basis for systems of oppression.[5] The concept of separate races, including ideas of inferiority and superiority, suited many as a justification for slavery and colonisation. It therefore contributed to economic privilege for white Europeans, the product of which is still with us.

Today race is understood as 'socially constructed'. Race is an idea that exists in society, but an idea that is so deeply entrenched that it just cannot be ignored. It has a real impact on people's lives.

"What is going on here, in large part, is that 'race' is not a clear, pre-existing, and self-evident category based on innate biology. Instead, categories of race, or racial identities, are the ongoing, living embodiments of history and of material and structural relations. Categories of race and racial identities are also embodiments of the political, social and moral agency (capacity for choice) that people live in, through, and in response to those histories and material and structural relations. This is the phenomenon scholars refer to when they claim race is a social construction."[6]

IF YOU STOP TALKING ABOUT RACE, RACISM WILL JUST GO AWAY

ERR ... NO ...

Colourblindness

Some people believe that if everyone were to recognise the fact that there is only one human race, issues of race and racism would disappear. Sometimes, people (particularly people of colour) who argue that race matters are themselves accused of being racist for identifying the distinction. Others (particularly white people) say society would be more just if we focus on what we have in common.

These approaches rest on a false assumption – that all people experience the world similarly. Pretending people of colour do not experience the world differently, when they tell us they do, denies their reality and allows white people to feel more secure in our own privilege. Whilst it is true that race is a concept that has been imagined by society, and not a natural or scientific concept, race is deeply rooted in society. Claiming to be colourblind, is to leave one of humanity's biggest injustices unchallenged.

Anti-racism advocates can find themselves being criticised for promoting an 'identity politics' that only divides people, including in otherwise progressive movements, like feminism. The identity politics framework is already dominant however, it is a politics shaped by an unspoken, subtle but powerful system of white identity and privilege that assumes whiteness in the norm. Colourblindness "denies racism and this holds it in place".[7] It can be well intentioned, but it does not interrupt racism, whilst making it more difficult for societies to address unconscious beliefs.

Some people of colour also reject race and say they are not disadvantaged by racism. We all have our own truth and lives that are affected by many factors.[8] We cannot assume that every member of any group that we perceive to be marginalised feels the same way.[i]

> *"I have come to realise that racism is not simply another name for racial prejudice, it is racial prejudice reinforced by power and privilege. Few people will comfortably admit to racism because it has become equated with fascism. Yet in truth racism encompasses a spectrum of behaviour that includes both thoughtless, uninformed white liberalism and the brutal horror of ethnic cleansing... ...Many Quakers have a problem with power; we like to be thought of as meek. But to avoid acknowledging powerfulness is to exert power without responsibility. In avoiding my own racism I am aligning myself with power and privilege. Jesus did not align himself with power and privilege."*
>
> — Ol (1994), *Quakers and race*, reprinted in *Rediscovering our Social Testimony (ROST): responses and challenges*.[9]

---

i. A person of colour consulted on this draft explained that sometimes people of colour adapt to racism by internalising it.

Racism

Racism is a system that advantages some and disadvantages others. It is a deeply rooted part of European society and structures that were shaped by the slave trade and colonisation. Racism is much more than psychological attitudes, false ideas about biology or hateful words and actions. Racism does not only affect all of us, it involves all of us.

Racism crosses the political spectrum and transcends the other good-bad frameworks that we use to make judgements about society. For example, race and racism are often ignored by many European social justice movements and advocates. Racism is not confined to the criminal justice system, but it is also about poverty, hunger, poor schooling, healthcare, safety and limited access to employment.

Racism can be seen in our daily lives. We see it when the TV news expresses more surprise at crimes taking place in white majority areas, and when TV advertisements perpetuate white notions of beauty. We see it in the absence of a sense of loss amongst white Europeans who do not have many friends of colour.[10] It affects the money in our pocket and the ways we spend our time.

RACISM

"Racism is a form of oppression in which one racial group dominates others. Oppression is group prejudice and discrimination backed by institutional power." [11]

PREJUDICE

"Learned prejudgement based on stereotypes about a social group. Prejudice occurs at the individual level. All human have learned prejudice." [12]

DISCRIMINATION

"Unfair action toward a social group and its members that is based on prejudice about the group. Discrimination occurs at the individual level. All humans discriminate."

What does research tell us about how people experience Europe differently?

If you have never experienced being followed by staff in a shop to ensure that you are not shoplifting, if you have never been asked where you are really from, if you've never seen a positive lead character in a film or book that looks like you, if you are generally trusted by strangers, and if you are never asked to account for the actions of someone else from your ethnic group (for example, after a terrorist attack), it may be difficult to recognise a different experience reported by others.

Research undertaken by the ICM polling company in 2018 surveyed the experiences of people living in the UK for The Guardian newspaper.[13]

- 14% of people of colour had been wrongly suspected of shoplifting in the last month, compared to 4% white people.

- People of colour were twice as likely as white people to have been mistaken for staff in restaurants, bars or shops.

- 20% of people of colour said they changed their appearance or voice because of their ethnicity.

- 41% of people of colour said someone had assumed that they were not British in the previous 12 months because of their ethnicity.

- 43% of people of colour felt they had been overlooked for a work promotion in the last 5 years in a way that felt unfair, compared to 18% of white people surveyed.

- 12% of people of colour had heard racist language directed at them within a month prior to the survey.

In their analysis the Guardian reported on other research that showed:

- White people found photos of black faces more threatening than photos of white people with the same expression.

- University professors were far more likely to respond to emails from students with white-sounding names.

The European Union Agency for Fundamental Rights (FRA) also published the results of a survey in 2018. The FRA research involved almost six thousand people of African decent living in twelve EU countries.

The research found that of the people of African decent that participated:

- 21% reported receiving racial harassment in the 12 months prior to the survey.

- 86% of people suffering harassment did not report it to any authority.

- 3% had been violently attacked.

- 11% of people suffering violent attacks said the perpetrator was a law enforcement official.

- Twice as many graduates of African descent were employed in manual work compared to graduates a whole.

- 14% say they were prevented from renting by a private landlord, and 6% by a social or municipal landlord. Perhaps partly as a result, 45% of people of African descent in Europe live in overcrowded accommodation, compared to 17% in the population as a whole.

This particular piece of FRA research focuses on Afrophobic prejudiced, discrimination and oppression, but they have undertaken other research which describes the extent of other forms of racism, including Anti-Semitism and Anti-Muslim discrimination.

So to recap, if you are never stopped by the police in your own neighbourhood, and the cultural norms at your school, or workplace, are the same as your home, these statistics may be a surprise and it may be difficult to understand how perceptions of race restrict other people's lives.

"Racism, Islamophobia and anti-Semitism are structural relations of inequality and exclusion, historically produced and embedded in institutional arrangements, and tied to larger processes of material exploitation. As such, they are not simply attitudes, perceptions, or feelings which can be remedied through education and enlightenment. But they nonetheless do directly affect how people see, feel, and inhabit the world, insinuating themselves into individuals' embodied dispositions and habits, their modes of interaction, discussion and representation. Racism, Islamophobia and anti-Semitism are expressed in words as well as deeds, through spoken and written signs, in gesture and fashion, in anger as well as solidarity. And signs, like words, do things. They tear people apart and bring them together. They exclude and include." [15]

— Paul Silverstein

When asking what makes racism so hard for white people to see, Robin DiAngelo points to the good-bad binary that operates. Suggesting that when someone is associated with racism they are likely to feel personally accused of being fundamentally immoral and therefore very defensive. If as a white person I understand racism through a binary and see myself as not racist, then what further work is required of me?[14]

White privilege

As some people face disadvantages, others are advantaged or privileged. A significant proportion of Europeans are people of colour,[16] meaning that when we see few or no people of colour in a place or an activity, then there are probably structures and processes that are excluding them.[i] The reasons for the exclusion might be subtle and difficult for people within the group to see. The reasons may be cultural, economic or something else that we do not understand and we feel we cannot change.

Being white means being identified by society as the top of the hierarchy of racial categories, and therefore "granted social, cultural, institutional, psychological and material advantages".[17] Most white people experience their privilege unconsciously, able to live in communities that reinforce the belief that their identity is neutral, normal, without a race.[18] This is different to the experience of people of

---

i. This book provides examples for the European Commission and the Religious Society of Friends.

colour, and is known as white privilege.

It is normal for white people to feel some resistance to this argument, and to fear what it means to be part of a racist system from which we benefit. We might also fear the change that may be needed to be more inclusive, or to live in a just world.

Remember whiteness is a powerful social creation. When white people talk about their skin colour they are more likely to refer to its colour as pale, pink, or maybe some shade of orange. The artificiality of white identity has often been close to the surface. For example, it was once possible for people of mixed heritage living in Spanish colonies to buy a certificate of whiteness.[19] In recent centuries groups have been reclassified as either white or non-white.

However, it is essential that white Europeans come to terms with the 'white' label. When we do not acknowledge whiteness and white privilege, we misunderstand racism as a problem pertaining primarily to people of colour. **When we realise that we are white and that this identity has an impact on our human relationships and how we move through the world, we can take responsibility for the privilege (or agency) we are afforded.**[20]

In many cases, it is difficult for white people to refuse the advantages that they receive. Realising that we are part of a system of white privilege, and extracting ourselves from that system is difficult. Even if we understand the advantages we receive, the price may be higher than we are prepared to pay. Anti-racism activists working with white people tell us that it is important to sit in this discomfort. Tenderness, patience and care for ourselves and others must also be part of any response.

Whiteness and community

Any unjust social phenomenon must be opposed, and even more so when it is so deeply entrenched that it is an accepted norm. As Diana Jeater said when talking about whiteness in her 2018 Salter lecture, "What do we want to unlearn? Who do we want to disempower? We can't be not white, so how do we want white to be?"

Individualism is a dominant part of European culture. It claims that there are no intrinsic boundaries to individual success, and denies the advantages of being white, such as the accumulation of wealth over generations. Individualism separates us from our neighbour and reduces our compassion to their suffering. For example, Michelle Alexander has undertaken research on mass incarceration and describes how one of the major challenges for racial justice is getting people to care about the incarceration of low-income ethnic minorities.[21] So part of whiteness is lack of compassion, but not to our friends or our children or the children of other white people, but to people of colour.

White privilege and political power

QCEA is based in Brussels, one of the global cities where power and privilege are negotiated. Racism is poorly understood and white privilege is not acknowledged amongst the political and diplomatic patchwork of policy discussions in Brussels.

Despite people of colour comprising about ten percent of the population for many western European countries, the European Commission employs very, very few people of colour, and refuses to allow any data collection about that number. Those elected to represent Europe's people are little better. Of the 751 Members of the European Parliament, only three are Black. European policy is informed and shaped by regular panel discussions. During one month in 2017 the gender and ethnicity of panellists in foreign policy events was monitored. Of 126 panellists, only one quarter were women, and NONE were people of colour.

Following interviews with people of colour working in the institutions, Michaela Benson and Chantelle Lewis (2019) found that people of colour often find themselves "as the only Black or Brown face in the room, [leading to a] lack of reckoning with colonial histories, and use of racial slurs in the workplace".[22]

In September 2016 a EurActiv journalist asked Alexander Winterstein (the Commission's deputy chief spokesperson) about ethnic diversity and was told that racial diversity did not need to be monitored as recruitment to the Commission was open to anyone to apply.[23] In 2017 the European Commission developed its Diversity and Inclusion Charter. The strategy includes measures to support workplace diversity in terms of age, disability, gender and LGBTI. Race is included in the opening statement within a longer list of characteristics, but it is not identified as a specific issue requiring attention.[24] Quakers joined with other Christian, Hindu, Jewish, Muslim, Sikh groups and anti-racist, LGBTI, disability and women's groups to write publicly to the Commissioner, but no change of direction looks likely.

The failure to recruit people of colour[i] is far more significant than just the EU institutions setting a bad example or missing out on talented people, but has real consequences for the culture and experience amongst the people that develop policy. To be institutions that serve all EU citizens, they need to include a spectrum of life experiences. As we have seen above, European citizens do not have similar or equal experiences of living here – and as things stand a monoethnic workforce is simply reinforcing privilege.[ii]

Being anti-racist is an expression of truth

In 1919 the Quaker William Braithwaite wrote:

"Evils which have struck their root deep in the fabric of human society are often accepted, even by the best minds, as part of the providential ordering of life. They lurk unsuspected in the order of things."[25]

---

i. One exception is that the European Commission and European Parliament organise traineeships that reach out to Roma candidates

ii. Many anti-racists would argue that recruiting People of Colour into existing organisations that have been used to reinforce privilege can only have a limited impact.

Socialisation

"Everyone receives value-laden racial messages daily that circulate in society; they are all around us ... While some of the messages are blatant (racist jokes, for example), we must understand that most of the messages we receive (and broadcast ourselves) are subtle and often invisible (especially to white people)." [26]

Textbooks, media, advertising, teachers and role models reduce the European history of slavery and colonialism to a footnote. Everyday conversations about which are the good parts of town, the good schools, etc. have an unspoken link to race. Common norms and standards of beauty emphasise the white body image, such as straight hair. Many popular TV shows are centred around all white friendship groups in racially diverse cities.[27]

People of colour receive the opposite message, as Alaka explains, "At 5 years old we are already conscious of the offence caused by our black body turning up in the wrong place and have begun to internalise the negative ideas about blackness so present in our culture".[28]

For several decades an experiment has assessed the age at which children receive signals about racial hierarchy. Psychologists Mamie and Kenneth Clarke developed the doll test, which gives children a sample of dolls. The dolls are identical except in skin tone. The children are asked which is the most/least beautiful, which they would most/

least like to look like, and which they would most like to have friends that looked like. The experiment has been conducted in several European countries (watch the Italian example linked in the footnote).[29] All children regardless of their colour strongly favour the doll representing white skin tone, and associate the doll representing black skin tone with being most undesirable.

"Any parent of black children growing up in a predominantly white society will tell you that their children become aware of racial hierarchy as soon as they start to attend nursery or playgroup. In the case of my three sons, each one of them demonstrated their awareness in different ways around the age of 3."
— Black European Quaker contributing to this book

Unpalatable truths

The invention of race

Groups of people often define themselves through their difference from other groups. However, the belief that permanently and naturally distinct groups of humans exist is a recent and very uncommon idea in human thought.[30]

The concept of race was spread through the 'European Enlightenment' of the 1700s.[31] One of the earliest identifiable descriptions of race can be found in the 1684 publication, *'Nouvelle division de la terre par les différents espèces ou races qui l'habitent'* (New division of Earth by the different species or races which inhabit it) by François Bernier. The following hundred years saw distinct racial groups being constructed through pseduo-science and other philosophical and cultural publications. Kant and other writers claimed that different body types represented different racial categories of human and assigned these categories particular characteristics (active/lazy, civilised/uncivilised, etc).[32]

The concept of different races was not just created out of scientific ignorance. It was deliberately created and manipulated to divide labourers who were resisting oppression from elites. The idea took hold with the rise of the transatlantic slave trade. Separating people of colour from us by telling dehumanising stories allowed white people to do terrible things, (take land, kill and enslave) and feel justified.

Missing histories: slavery and race

What were we taught at school about the 16th, 17th, 18th and 19th Centuries? Did we learn about industrial revolutions that took place in Europe, and the white men that built businesses, invented machines or discovered new worlds? Students often learn about the European weaving industries, with little reference to the cheap cotton used in Europe, sold by traders in the northern states of the USA, and produced by enslaved people in the southern states.

Slavery has existed in different times in history with particular groups or individuals dominating others. However, it was during the last 400 years that slaves were used on a massive scale to create wealth by taking and harvesting natural resources from the land as cheaply as possible. In total, about 10.5 million Africans arrived in the Americas.[33] A further 1.5 million died on board slave ships en route from Africa, and more millions died in forced marches from inland areas to coastal ports.

The transatlantic slave trade was also compounded by the degree to which it dehumanised people, treating them as a completely expendable commodity. It is also the massive scale of displacement and the capitalist legacy that is so damaging.

Many Europeans work to improve the well-being of their societies, but we underestimate the impact of slavery and Europe's colonial history on present day wellbeing. Most Europeans are taught only about European history and the history of Europeans (often exclusively men) in other parts of the world. When we exclude people of colour from history, we exclude them from a shared present and future.

"When I was at primary school in the 1990s I learned about 'Christopher Columbus discovering America'. It was acknowledged that there were of course people already there, but I did not learn any of their names. At secondary school I watched Roots and learned about the slave trade, but I do not remember the names of any African people's that existed before the slave trade."

— Participant at QCEA anti-racism course, Feb 2019

Some often-overlooked historical facts include:

- There were African histories before the slave trade and colonialism.

- The truth of African resistance is rarely told, but it is estimated that about one million more people would have been taken from Africa were it not for defensive actions to damage slave ships and attacks on kidnappers. British, French and Dutch records show 483 such actions on the West African coast.[34]

- The treatment of people of African descent in north America was less brutal at first, but got worse as the concept of race and the systems of white supremacy were developed. As Quaker academic Jeff Hitchcock explains "The earliest Africans in [north] America were understood by Europeans in America to be humans, with souls".[35]

- The slave trade was not one unfortunate event but a legal system upheld by Europeans and people of European descent over centuries that supported the intergenerational transfer of wealth between certain people.[36]

- Dehumanising images of people of colour were brought to populations on an industrial scale to justify the colonial enterprise conducted in their name. Colonial activities included, taking land, maiming, killing, enslaving, separating parents from children, forbidding use of languages, erasing lineage through bureaucracy, and much more.

To consider your education by reading some snapshots of the history of European colonialism and how the system of racism was invested, please see appendix A.

The legacy of the 19th Century lives on today

In 1800, before the Industrial Revolution, Europeans controlled at least 35 percent of land worldwide, but this was 84 percent by 1914. It was in this later period that Europeans were particularly subject to imperialist propaganda – art, music and education. Huge exhibitions were effective tools for explaining the virtues of colonialism to the public. Examples include the British Empire exhibition held at Wembley Park (1924-5), and the colonial section of the Brussels International Exposition (1897). The Belgian exposition was notable due to the almost eight million people who attended, and its recreation of a Congolese village (human zoo), in which 267 African people were incarcerated. Seven died during their time in captive display.[37] Following World War II,[i] the European colonial system was disrupted with nearly all Europe's colonies gaining political independence between 1945 and 1975 – in some cases after devastating wars (e.g. Angola).[38]

The 19th Century was an important century for European thought, significantly shaping concepts and systems of politics, economics, science and much more. This extended quote from Valentin-Yves Mudimbe explains how deeply ideas of race are embedded in the institutions

---

i. Millions of people of colour (from colonies and African Americans) serviced in the military and civil forces of European countries during World War II.

and narratives that shape our lives today.

"The problem is that during this period both imperialism and anthropology took shape, allowing the reification of the 'primitive'. The key is the idea of History with a capital H, which first incorporates Saint Augustine's notion of providence and later on expresses itself in the evidence of Social Darwinism. Evolution, conquest, and difference become signs of a theological, biological, and anthropological destiny, and assign to things and beings both their natural slots and social mission. Theorists of capitalism, such as Benjamin Kidd and Karl Pearson in England, Paul Leroy-Beaulieu in France, Friedrich Naumann and Friedrich von Bernhard in Germany, as well as philosophers, comment upon two main and complementary paradigms. These are the inherent superiority of the white race, and, as already made explicit in Hegel's Philosophy of Right, the necessity for European economies and structures to expand to 'virgin areas' of the world." [39]

Europe and decolonisation

Subjugation and impoverishment are the building blocks of European colonial wealth. During the post-war period many of the territories controlled by European colonial powers became independent states. European governments then introduced guest worker schemes and mass recruitment from former colonies that diversified the populations of many countries, such as the UK, France and Belgium. This immigration made a significant contribution to European economic growth during the formative years

31

of the European Union project. However, at the same time these communities were often portrayed as a burden on European societies.

Between 1962-1981 Britain passed a series of laws that removed British citizenship from people of colour from the Commonwealth, making it more difficult for people of colour to migrate to Britain whist not affecting the freedom white Australians, South Africans and New Zealanders had to do so.[40]

In 2011 a British court heard a legal action brought by survivors of British concentration camps in Kenya in 1950s. The legal action helped to reveal 'Operation Legacy' that during the period of decolonisation destroyed British colonial records that could be used to damage the British colonial reputation in the future. Some records dated as far back as 1662.[41]

Slavery and colonialism represent a huge transfer of wealth from one people to another. As Jennifer Harvey argues:

"The implications of this [history] and its meaning should shake us to our core; this is a difficult and potentially reality-changing truth with which those of us who are White need to tarry and attempt to absorb deeply ... For this legacy bequeaths a crisis that resides in our very bodies and demands responses from us that are radically different from those we have collectively made to this point."[42]

Colonial propaganda and Afrophobia today

Approximately 13 million people of African descent live in Europe. The fear, dislike or hatred of people of African descent is known as Afrophobia, a specific form of racism that receives little public or official attention.

Afrophobic prejudice is linked to discrimination in education, health care, the labour market, justice systems and the media. In particular, young Black men are disproportionately represented negatively in newspapers, TV news, music videos and computer games. Black men are too often featured in supporting roles alongside white protagonists. They are also stereotyped in criminal and violent roles, using similar imagery to that used during European colonisation to claim that African men were wild and needed European civilisation.

Sweden

Research commissioned by the Swedish Minister of Integration in 2013 showed that stereotypes dating back to colonialism were still prominent in Swedish culture. The report concluded that Swedes of African descent are marginalised in social, economic and political terms. The research also identified the presence of Afrophobia within society.

Netherlands and Belgium

Colonial imagery continues to be used on our continent. One high profile example is the character of 'Zwarte Piet' that has been used to perpetuate racist stereotypes since the 1850s and is still celebrated in the Netherlands and Flanders every December.[43] This example is just one consequence of failing to address Europe's historically harmful relationship with other parts of the world, and failing to acknowledge how it continues to influence society and politics today.

Football

Black players continue to sometimes face racist chants during football matches. This sometimes takes the dehumanising form of imitation monkey noises or bananas thrown onto the pitch. When these incidents are discussed publicly, the European origins of this association are not discussed, avoiding a history of human zoos, mentioned above.[44]

Trauma

QCEA's 2015 publication Hate Crime: Prevention and Restoration in the EU, reported that victims of Afrophobic hate crime have more severe feelings of powerlessness and insecurity than hate crime victims as a whole. This is thought to be due to the long history of structural disadvantage against people of African descent. Police violence is an important component of Afrophobic violence in Europe, which can have long-lasting impacts on how survivors relate to the state and understand their citizenship.

Portrayals of development in Africa

Collectively, the EU has the largest international development budget in the world. However, it is much smaller than the financial flows that are transferred to the global south by the African, Asian and Latin American diaspora communities. As Diana Jeater reminds us, "Let us think of Africans as donors, because actually they are. The flow of wealth flows into us, we just give a little bit of it back".[45]

The challenge for white people is to de-centre ourselves from our Eurocentric world view. This means reading African and other non-European historians, writers, journalists, and histories of resistance to colonialism.

Missing histories: Islam in Europe

Anti-migrant attitudes are built upon narratives of outsiders coming to already-constituted and stable European nations, rather than recognising the history of people of colour as part of Europe and European identity. The narrative is one of white as normal, and people of colour as outsiders or invaders.

During 2015 when many people were fleeing Syria and Iraq, former Romanian President Traian Basescu said, "I think about the problem in terms of national security. Let us not forget that among these people are Sunni, Shia, people who put bombs reciprocally in their country (...) Why should we Islamise Europe? We should destroy the migrants' boats and ships, right in the docks. Otherwise immigration will increase each year, will triple from year to year".[46]

The 'Muslim invasion' narrative has been increasingly used by far-right political groups in Europe in recent years, and a softer version of the same narratives can be deployed by mainstream politicians. The success of this narrative is boosted by an ignorance about Islam and its historical presence in a Europe that is portrayed as being permanently and homogeneously Christian.

Germany

In March 2018 Germany's Interior Minister, Horst Seehofer, told the Bild newspaper that Islam did not belong in Germany. He was criticised by German Chancellor Angela Merkel, but refused to withdraw the statement. About 3 percent of German citizens are Muslim, but estimates suggest that they are significantly over-represented in the German prison population. Muslims have been part of the German population since at least the 18th Century, when some were known to have served in the army. A Muslim cemetery was established in Berlin in 1798.

France

Muslims have been present in France since the 8th century, including the Umayyad in parts of southern France repeatedly until the 10th century.[47] During the colonial period France forcibly governed millions of Muslims in North and West Africa (directly, e.g. Algeria, or indirectly, e.g. Tunisia and Morocco). Part of the claim that Islam is incompatible with France is based on the idea that the country does not distinguish between the public and private realm, and therefore between religion and politics. This argument overlooks the fact that like early Christians, many of today's Christians do not accept that distinction, however they are also not targeted in the same way as Muslim communities are.[i]

Finally, it is worth noting that anti-Muslim narratives have continued to spread despite significant white European Muslim populations, such as in Bosnia-Herzegovina.

I the metro driver,
was a Muslim like so many of the others
you never hear
you never see
But of whom there are oh-so many.

— Poem by Mohamed El Bachiri, whose wife was killed in the Brussels bombing of March 2016

---

i. Many Quakers in France are actively engaged in politics, for example through their vocal opposition to the Eurosatory international arms fairs in Paris.

Race and belonging in Europe today

Football player Mesut Özil annouched in 2018 that he would not play for Germany again, pointing to his racist treatment by the German football federation and print media. "I am German when we win but I am an immigrant when we lose", he said in a statement. Soon afterwards, England player Raheem Sterling drew attention to racism in the UK media. Sterling said the print media fuel racism by covering the private lives of young black players in a different manner to their white counterparts.[48]

Research about France has found that the media uses signifiers of national origin to describe people of colour.[49] Silverstein argued, "Discourse that labels certain Muslim-French citizens as second or third generation immigrants, as if they carry foreignness in their genealogy, is ultimately a racialising gesture of exclusion". In 2019 the preliminary report of a UN expert group visiting Belgium found that, "Public officials consistently rationalised systemic exclusion of people of African decent with references to language and culture, even in cases involving second generation Belgians".[50] These examples of othering show the limited inclusion Europe is willing to offer.

The lives and imaginations of young people whose parents or grandparents migrated to Europe are not limited to national boundaries. Some white people find this such a challenge to European national identities that they characterise people who express these international connections as a problem that needs to be dealt with, through institutional, legal or policing control.[51]

Colonialism has locked Europeans into economically dependent relationships with indigenous populations of the lands Europe occupied. French anti-racism thinker Albert Memmi wrote in 1991 that people of colour are partly a "living reminder of Europe's colonial enterprise ... an unpaid debt contracted in sweat and blood".[52]

In his study of postcolonial France, Paul Silverstein asks how people of colour, "make spaces of social, cultural, religious, and political exclusion, like the housing projects of the Parisian banlieues, their own? How do they construct rich, meaningful, and flourishing lives for themselves in such places?"[53] Memmi argues that there is limited hope for many people of colour who are structurally marginalised, "Europe offers no hopeful vision, but only either reactive policing or resigned complacency".[54]

Colonial relationships between Europe and other parts of the world were developed before today's Europeans were born, but we are responsible when our politics accepts and extends the privilege of some at the expense of others.

RACE
IS ABOUT SOCIAL RELATIONS FORGED THROUGH
COLONIAL VIOLENCE
AND
REPRODUCED
FOR
CONTROL & PROFIT
THROUGH LAWS, INSTITUTIONS AND OTHER SYSTEMS

Exclusion policy today

All of us know deep down that there is no 'other'. We are all part of one common human family, and one shared ecosystem that belongs to none of us. However in recent years Europe's political discourse has been increasingly influenced by 'us and them', with a stronger focus on Europe's external border.

The dominance of migration in European political discourse is deeply intertwined with questions of race. We need to remember that there are tens of millions of refugees worldwide and a tiny proportion are hosted in Europe. As Mehdi Hasan has said, "Obsessing over Europe's refugee crisis while ignoring Africa's is white privilege at work".[55]

We have seen the construction of walls and fences to keep people from reaching safe territory (in breach of international obligations to shelter refugees), with prominent examples on Hungary's southern border, France's border with the UK, and most recently on Croatia's border with Bosnia-Herzegovina. Another example of the harmful consequences of the othering of migrants and refugees has been the frequency of immigration detention. European governments are increasingly using detention as a means of more efficiently returning failed asylum seekers to their country of origin.[56]

Despite migration into Europe having now reduced to pre-2015 levels, the impact of the 2015 political crisis and its legacy on future EU budgets will be significant. The proposed EU budget framework (or Multi-Annual Financial Framework) allocates unprecedented levels of funding for border management and military projects over the next seven years. This includes €21bn for external border control, and another €21bn for arms research, development and procurement. In both cases this is many times what has been spent in the last seven years. Since 2015 European governments have already deployed joint naval operations through the European Union Common Security and Defence Policy in the Mediterranean and through NATO in the Aegean Seas.[57] There is evidence that alternative policies could be implemented, and QCEA is one of several organisations advocating for these.[58]

European governments are increasingly diverting development aid to pay for militarisation in countries on the migrant path to Europe. A migration-security-industry has developed, with significant lobbying influence in Brussels and other European capitals. European governments seek to use many tools to persuade other countries to host migrants or accept people being returned whose asylum applications have been rejected. Such policies include direct payments, manipulation of trade agreements and new conditions for the receipt of development aid. Notable examples include the EU-Turkey deal and EU funding for the Libyan coast guard (which Amnesty International has said amounts to EU complicity in torture).

How might governments respond?

Many anti-racist activists are sceptical about the impact of engagement with political institutions, believing that justice and equality require fundamental political and economic change. Whilst the increasing importance of collective European policy making represents a sensible approach to common challenges for many, a strong 'Europeanness' is understood by others to be a racial project that produces a European polity that identifies as Christian and white.[59]

However, there are many specific policies that privilege some and disadvantage others, and these can be challenged as we seek to reduce greater systemic harm. For QCEA, protecting and promoting international and European law on racial equality, and working to address institutional barriers to racial justice in European structures are necessary parts of working on Quaker concerns, particularly as we seek to change Europe's response to people seeking sanctuary.

There are many specific policies that could be changed to make our continent and world more racially just. A few examples include:

- Providing development assistance on the basis of need and ending the coercion of non-European countries to restrict migration, in ways (such as arbitrary detention) that are likely to lead to human rights violations.

- Holding to account governments that are inciting hatred toward migrants, ignoring violence toward people of colour, or otherwise not meeting the standards of the EU Charter of Fundamental Rights.[60] Progress can be made by EU member states using EU infringement proceedings.

- Monitoring levels of inclusion and discrimination in all aspects of European, national and local policy.[61]

- Introducing an EU framework to support each country to create a national afrophobia strategy. This has been requested by a UN body, but no European country has produced a strategy so far. A first step could be to follow Sweden's example and commission specific research into afrophobia nationally or locally. Equivalent strategies could follow for other forms of prejudice.

"The European standpoint on migration utilises control under white supremacy, neoliberalism and patriarchal hegemony, the effects of which manifest into criminalisation of migration, and of people of colour. We must not only call for no borders, no deportations, no detentions as an attempt to redistribute power, but call for the end of such prevailing superiority."

— Part of a Statement by the Black Dissidents group at the DSEi Arms Fair in London, September 2015

"Historical injustice creates a particular kind of world. It doesn't stop when colonialism stopped. We are born into a world that was made by historical injustice. It's the world we still live in. And just because we are good and kind and mean well, it doesn't mean we are excused from, or above, or apart from the systems of privilege that shape our world. So we may have misunderstandings, but where the responsibility for putting those right lies I think is not equally balanced." [62]

— Diana Jeater, Salter Lecture, 2018

Like gender, race is a "structural condition of the modern world ... internalised in bodily dispositions ... inscribed in lived social relations and everyday encounters. They produce durable inequalities that have the effect of social reality even if they fail the scientific tests of contemporary biology or the ethical aspirations of liberal sensibilities." [63]

— Paul Silverstein

"In the end human rights are about people being treated and feeling like people who matter. We are reminded graphically of violations of human rights far away and near at hand. In ignorance or knowingly we all violate human rights. We are all involved in the exercise and abuse of power." [64]

— London Yearly Meeting (Quakers in Britain, 1986)

Groups openly committed to racism

The theme of this book is that racism and white supremacy are much more than the tradition neo-Nazi or skinhead caricature. However, white supremacist groups do exist, and are increasingly emboldened in many parts of Europe. These groups use the concept of 'the other' to reinvent a narrative of national identity through which they privilege particular groups within society, such as the current elite, or a far-right political group seeking power.[i]

Research published by the European Network Against Racism reported the growth in European political forces that aim to privilege the interests of people who are perceived to be the native population.[65] French far-right leader Marine Le Pen seems to agree having called 2016, "the year the Anglo-Saxon world woke up".[66]

Openly racist narratives are regularly heard within political discussion. Recent examples include a Danish politician who argued that only white people can be Danish and a Polish Member of the European Parliament (MEP) that referred to migrants travelling to Europe as 'human garbage' whilst speaking in the Parliament's chamber.[67]

Politicians who promote ethnic-nationalism exploit the fear that governments cannot protect citizens from globalisation. For example, in 2015, the Hungarian government launched a billboard campaign that featured

i. Often described as nationalism, nativism, or the broader term populism.

messages such as, "If you come to Hungary, you cannot take away Hungarians' jobs". The billboards were written in Hungarian and could only reasonably be expected to increase fear of migrants as they could not be read by people who did not know Hungarian. The public campaign also included questionnaires that attributed forced migration to EU membership and linked migration with terrorism.[68] There are plenty of western European examples with similar 'hostile environment' style policies, including recent interior ministers of France and UK: Nicolas Sarkozy, David Blunkett and Theresa May.

Nationalistic populism has been identified as a distinctive feature of recent years by the Council of Europe's expert body,[69] the European Commission against Racism and Intolerance (ECRI).[70] The body monitors racism in Europe and prepares recommendations for the Council of Europe's 47 member states. Recent annual reports have included the following concerns:

- Hate speech is not confined to extreme groups but also found in the political mainstream.

- Women wearing visible religious symbols (especially headscarves) have been particularly targeted.

- Despite efforts of some countries' authorities to address the barriers for Roma people to obtain personal identity documents given the nature of their housing arrangements, they continued to suffer from widespread prejudice, stigma, violence and social exclusion.

- People of African descent continue to experience racist abuse, including the prominent example of abuse of Black football players.

Brexit hate, not so new

Brexit discussions are a useful vehicle for some far-right groups to try to build wider public support. For example, activists linked to the English Defence League sought and failed to trigger a #YellowJacketsUK street campaign with themselves at the helm.

There has been much discussion of an increase in hate crime following the Brexit referendum. The accounts of people experiencing hostility due to their nationality (or perceived nationality) whilst living in Britain in the year after the referendum have been widely heard.

However, racism is not an aberration in Britain linked to Brexit. According to Akwugo Emejulu, following her research into the operation of white supremacy before and after the EU referendum, many social justice campaigners are too quick to claim "This is not who we are", without examining the wider system of racism of which they are part.

Akwugo Emejulu argues that:

"An unstated campaign strategy of the Leave campaign was to re-imagine Britain and Britishness (but really Englishness) as white in order to make particular kinds

of claims to victimhood which would highlight economic inequality without challenging neoliberalism. For instance, a key argument of the campaign was that the 'working class' (who were unquestionably assumed to be white) were suffering under the burden of mass immigration, which transformed the culture of their neighbourhoods and put undue strain on public services."[71]

Research by Michaela Benson and Chantelle Lewis (2019) further supports this argument, analysing the perspectives of people of colour in the UK and in the EU-27. The research finds that their views on Brexit are shaped by their frequent pre-referendum experience of racism – so that Brexit is more a continuation of the norm than it is an abortion. For example, a person of colour living on the European mainland, explained, "What has transpired in Britain since the Leave campaign won has only shown how easily the veneer of civility and conviviality can be peeled back to reveal the virulence of racism and xenophobia seething under the skin of British social life."[72]

Wealth and class privilege can also create blind spots in our understanding of Brexit. Anthropologist Terrance Turner (1995) argues that support for anti-migrant and xenophobic politics are as much about racial exclusion as they are for a call for inclusion by white working-class people who are suffering from post-industrial economic changes, a European community in which they do not seem to have a place.[73]

Communities need to come together to mend the many

tears in our social fabric, overcoming far-right politics through solidarity. However it is not inevitable that this will happen. As Alaka argues, "Pretending that Europe is now so enlightened and democratic that the pogroms against outsiders that have characterised much of its history prior to 1945 cannot return is pure delusion".[74]

Our place in community

This section continues to speak to white people involved in social justice, peace or faith based activities. How can we live in community with people of colour when we benefit from inequality and privilege, and we do not take risks to challenge structural racism, and we do not take significant steps to share power, and therefore disempower ourselves?

We can all speak up for racial justice within the movements of which we are already a part. Political, social, and faith-based organisations, businesses and trade unions must all do more to identify and support anti-racism groups to broaden the coalition of groups addressing racism. White privilege is a test of whether as traditional peace and social justice groups we are willing and able to reach out beyond our current constituencies. This applies to European and north American Quaker organisations and many of our traditional allies and partners.

As white people growing in concern for anti-racism, we naturally face the question 'what can we do?'. As we search for what love requires of us, we may find some surprising answers. It may not be activity, and it is unlikely to be leadership. This can feel strange if we are used to being part of a privileged group, and being influential in group settings. This is because there is a real risk of doing harm, repeating the practices and behaviour of the dominant group, and therefore furthering rather than undermining racism.

A crucial step on a journey to understand what it means to be white will be understanding the harm of white privilege. The Quaker Peace and Social Witness booklet *'Power and Privilege'* (2018) gives advice about sitting with the discomfort comes with a growing awareness of privilege.[75] The booklet says:

- Learn to recognise when you are finding listening to others' concerns difficult, and then learn to manage your reaction.

- Resist the urge to move the topic onto 'safer' territory.

White role to support, not lead

For white people that are new to anti-racism it is important not to be overconfident, for example by undertaking well-meaning forms of anti-racist activism that are in fact not appreciated by people of colour. As many anti-racism activists have said, it is not the responsibility of people of colour to educate society about racism. This is why if you go to an anti-racism conference you may find that time is allowed for people of colour and white people to meet separately (as a caucus).

White anti-racism author Shelly Tochluk's advice is to:

> *"Step back and listen,*
> *leave your guilt at the door,*
> *avoid appeals for affirmation,*
> *admit you do not know,*
> *stay in conversation,*
> *ensure that you are not taking over*
> *by talking too much*
> *or trying to lead without being asked,*
> *accept leadership from people of colour,*
> *don't be defensive,*
> *accept feedback*
> *interrupt racism and privilege when you see it...*
> *...be prepared to prove yourself over time*
> *in order to earn trust,*
> *[and] make a long-term commitment to a place*
> *(like a particular organisation or town) where*
> *you can nurture authentic relationships."*[76]

In addition to this list, it is important for white people to be aware that colonialism and racism pitted communities of colour against each other, and we must be vigilante so that we do not contribute to this.[i]

Anti-racism projects need financial support, and so fundraising and donating are also important ways that

---

i. Advice from person of colour providing feedback on this draft text.

we can contribute as individuals. Within local, national and international contexts, there are a different range of activities that individual citizens can undertake including, home-based research, human rights monitoring, advocacy with individuals and following up on specific human rights violations.

White anti-racist leadership might be more appropriate when activities focus on the education of white people. Every week, for more than a year, QCEA's race and privilege reading group has provided a space for people to share their experience and learn from a journey of racial awakening. We have also held a weekend course on the same theme. This is an example of white people coming together to work on our own racism.

Where the majority of participants in an anti-racism project are white, the project will often develop an accountability mechanism to ensure that it can be shaped by people of colour. It is important for any project to have a close relationship with people affected, but particularly in the context of white privilege. QCEA consulted with groups representing people of colour before establishing its reading group and has continued to provide updates and receive feedback.

White church

The history of the white Christian church in slavery, colonialism and racism includes some horrific crimes and perverted religious defence and justifications as this quote from King Leopold's Ghost shows:

"Thousands more children perished during the long journeys to get there. Of one column of 108 boys on a forced march to the state colony at Boma in 1892-1893, only sixty-two made it to there destination; eight of them died within the following few weeks. The mother superior of one Catholic colony for girls wrote to a high Congo state official in 1895, 'Several of the little girls were so sickly on their arrival that ... our good sisters couldn't save them, but all had the happiness of receiving Holy Baptism; **they are now little angels in Heaven who are praying for our great king'.**"[77]

"We pray that the 'scales will fall from our own eyes' and those of our politicians – as they did from Saul."

— From 3-5 February 2017, the Quaker Asylum and Refugee Network and other Quaker agencies held a conference, *Forced Migration: how can Quakers respond*, at Woodbrooke Quaker Study Centre in Birmingham, UK.

White majority faith communities are an important part of the landscape of white privilege. They can also be an important vessel for the uncomfortable journey of deconstructing white privilege. This section is written for white majority churches in general. The author has experience in Anglican and Methodist communities, but the reflections primarily rest in a Quaker experience.

> I AM WHITE, SO IS EVERYONE IN MY CHURCH. SO RACISM ISN'T DISCUSSED. IT'S NOT AN ISSUE HERE.

People of faith are called to ask deep questions. So why is it so difficult for us to think deeply about the history of our religious institutions? Why, for example, does so much religious iconography continue to be produced depicting Adam and Eve, other key Christian figures and even God as white?[78] Why has there been so little reflection by churches about our historic relationship with slavery, colonialism and racism? This section considers diversity and inclusion in white majority churches, the history of church institutions and what churches can do to change.

Homogeneity

Some liberal religious communities are active on social justice issues and outspoken about their belief in equality, whilst at the same time remaining racially homogeneous. Malcolm X described the most segregated hour in American life as high noon on Sunday, and a similar situation is found here.

In Europe black people have a higher level of church attendance than white people. However, they have often had to create their own churches due to the lack of inclusion in white majority churches. Other churches with more diversity have few people of colour in positions of leadership. Making efforts to reach out to a wider spectrum of society can be an exciting opportunity for community building and spiritual growth, however we must be open to change and not expect new people to simply conform to white church structures.

Faith communities often reflect on how welcoming we are to enquirers. One query is to ask whether we have any community practices that subtly exclude others. For example, if the photographs on our notice boards and in our newsletters are all of white people, what message might this give?

Jamie Bartlett's 2017 book, '*Radicals: Outsiders Changing the World*' includes some important reflections on the inclusiveness of social movements. Jamie describes his research with the far-right English Defence League, and with two different groups of environmental activists. Jamie found it easier to fit into the far-right group, as the environmental groups had developed specific cultural practices that helped long standing members to feel included in the group, but left new participants feeling excluded and judged as less virtuous.[79]

Faith communities have many specific religious and organisational forms that help to bind them together as a group. Perhaps the smaller and more radical the faith community is, the more particular and coded these cultural practices become.

White Quaker culture in Europe

In her research of Quakers of colour by the historically white led Quaker institutions in north America, Vanessa Julye found an article from an 1850 edition of Friends Review that notes the long commitment Quakers have had to advocacy on behalf of people of colour, but the very small numbers of people of colour who were members of the Religious Society of Friends. The article of 1850 asks, "Are they kept at a distance by our neglect or repulsive conduct?"[80]

The answer seems obvious when we consider reports from Quakers of colour about stereotyping when attending Quaker Meetings in Europe today. A Quaker of Asian decent reports that they were greeted at the door of a Quaker Meeting with a Buddhist Namaste bow with hands pressed together, when white Friends were greeted with a handshake. A southern African Quaker visiting Europe in 2018 was greeted at Sunday worship with a warning that European Quakers do not sing in Meeting. Despite this not even being true, the Friend was visiting from another unprogrammed Meeting, and was no more likely to brake into song than anyone else. Ignorance of the diversity of African Quakers and a lack of interest in their spirituality is a white suprematist attitude. Whilst these experiences will be in the wider context of more positive experiences from people of colour attending Quaker Meetings, we cannot ignore that this does happen.

There are also more inclusive elements of Quaker culture. Quaker Jeff Hitchcock, talking about Quakers of European descent and white culture, writes, "We share white cultural practices in some ways. Our faith can be highly individualistic. Unlike faiths in many other cultures, we do not impart spirituality to objects, places and ancestors. We tend to be rational and non-expressive. In other ways we tend to be out of step with white culture. We value our elders; we make collective decisions according to a process of consensus; we favour non-hierarchical and non-patriarchal social arrangements, and we do not believe that wealth proves one's goodness. We value simplicity."[81]

Churches making progress

Jennifer Harvey, author of the book 'Dear White Christians' argues that progress in white majority churches has come from self-criticism, in particular of our poor understanding of the concept of racism.[82] As we have said many times above, it is not about being mean, or bad words. Racism is a system of oppression which involves all of us.

In 1994 a pastoral letter from the House of Bishops of the Episcopal Church (USA) called on white people to take an inventory of places in which they participate in racist structures and begin to actively refuse such participation.[83] In 2006 the Episcopal Church as a whole agreed to work for legislation initiating the study of the legacy of slavery, and to produce its own study of the economic privileges derived from slavery. The Church directed every diocese to begin collecting detailed information about its particular history of complicity in the institution of slavery, in order to begin "repair[ing] the breach (Isaiah 58:12) both materially and relationally".[84]

In 2004 the Presbyterian Church (USA) Task Force to Study Reparations completed its report with a series of recommendations for confession, examining history and the results of a survey of lay people. The report said, "We live in hope that race and class prejudices will be overcome in our lifetimes. Yet we remain unwilling to acknowledge the sins of our fathers and mothers, as well as the fact that we receive residual benefits from the advantages that accrued to them because of their sins".[85] The report was approved by the church's General Assembly and study and worship resources were commissioned.

Cameroonian theologian Jean-Marc Ela calls on churches, "to be what they are called to be – the critical link between revelation and history, thus shaping a different world right here".[86] So where can Quakers begin in understanding our history?

Quaker history

Given the Quaker role in anti-racist activities such as anti-slavery campaigns, the Underground Railroad and the *Kindertransport*, it is important for European Quakers not to idolise Quaker history. For example, we cannot consider the ideas of William Penn – the proponent of mechanisms of peaceful cooperation in Europe – without recognising that he was also a slave holder.

A new book by Katherine Gerbner, *'Christian Slavery: Conversion and Race in the Protestant Atlantic World'* shows that Quakers in Barbados in the 1670s held slaves.[87] Quaker missionaries travelled there within ten years of the movement starting in England and many took on the Quaker identity, including two of the largest sugar farmers.Both held people as slaves, and they did not release their slaves upon their Quaker convincement. Half-hearted challenges to Quaker slaveholding from Quaker leaders George Fox and Richard Pinder missed the point. They argued that all people were part of the same human family and were equal in the sight of God, but they only asked slaveholders to be merciful, and not to free their captives. As Quaker communities became established in north America, some used connections in Barbados to traffic people of colour for slavery onto plantations in four US states.[88]

Quakers settling in north America from the Dutch-German

border areas led the first recorded protest by a community of white people against slavery (in 1688), and would go on to collectively condemn slavery before other European Christian denominations. However, racial injustice within Quaker communities continued to be expressed in other ways. In her 2009 book (*'Fit for Freedom, Not for Friendship: Quakers, African Americans and the myth of Racial Justice'*) written with Donna McDaniel, Vanessa Julye documents how people of colour were discriminated against within Quaker institutions in north America, for example in matters of membership, marriage and seating in Meeting Houses.[89]

"Friends have always understood that when we mismanage material affairs, we suffer spiritual harm. In other words, so long as the dominant culture in our nations continues to reap the material benefit of policies based on the historical theft and diversion of resources from [people of colour] our lives will continue to be distorted and we will not be able to attain the spiritual fullness of God's community here on Earth. Friends need to ask ourselves: What is our present spiritual condition? One cannot be passively nonracist in a society whose very economy has been structured on a racist past."[90]

— Jeff Hitchcock

Quakers also need to be careful not to overstate the Quaker role in the abolition of slavery in British Empire. Whilst Quakers were key figures in the British anti-slavery movement, histories of abolition often tell the story of white people involved in the parliamentary process.[i] It does not tell the much bigger story of slave resistance and rebellion.

What can we do?

Typical contributions faith communities can make include:

- Learning about the impact of racism.

- Calling for an apology from our governments and/or religious institutions for their role in colonialism.

- Researching people in our faith communities who benefited from slavery and how these benefits are still experienced today.

- Giving space and funding to people of colour in white majority faith communities to spend time by themselves where they can share their experiences and help each other repair the harm.[91]

- Measure the diversity in our church communities.

- Public statements.

- Offering sanctuary.

---

i. Britain was also, as is often claimed, not the first empire to ban slavery. Denmark banned it in 1792 and France did for a short time during the French Revolution in 1794.

- Financial support for anti-racism activity led by people of colour.

- Prayer.

In 2017 Britain's Quaker Peace and Social Witness launched a programme to encourage Quaker Meetings to more clearly serve as places of sanctuary. In just a year twenty percent of Quaker Meetings have decided that they wanted to take part. One of the activities that Quaker Meetings are undertaking is to offer their premises for free to anti-racism groups and events.

Anti-racism as a spiritual practice

Anti-racism activities will offer our communities opportunities for connection and growth. In her chapter 'Not Somewhere else, but here: the struggle for racial justice as a struggle to inhabit my country' Rebecca Parker imagines anti-racist activism as a spiritual practice that can enable us to reclaim our humanity from a life of "numbness and disengagement".[92]

This challenge may feel overwhelming, but it is necessary and presents opportunities for growth. We need to unlearn behaviours and assumptions we have as part of a group with privilege. We need to discover seeking racial justice as a spiritual practice.

QCEA Assistant Clerk (vice-chair) and Swiss Quaker Rorie Nazareth says, "It would be interesting to think of the spiritual practice in two ways. One is developing the capacity of self-awareness, as in talking about racism makes me deeply uncomfortable, defensive, angry, etc. Second is looking at working towards the structures that enforce equality as well as the internal, unconscious biases that drive the attitudes of racism that can persist even when there are laws against it".

"An early conception of human rights is implicit in the seventeenth century political and religious experience of [Quakers]. Such rights are inherent in the 'neighbour principle' as a source of social responsibility, common to world faiths." [93]

— Michael Bartlet

Religion shaped ideas ... Slaves were 'children' that needed to be told what to do, black bodies were uniquely suited to the hardest labour, having babies in the fields, etc. This was reflected in the Spanish genocide and conquer of Central, South America, and the Caribbean. English colonists to the New World saw 'savages' that needed to be civilised. They were acting according to rights given by God. But ultimately it was always about taking something from an other and not feeling guilty about it"

— Rorie Nazareth

PEACE

Racial injustice is violence

SIMPLICITY

We should not fear
diminished material standing

EQUALITY

We should be advocates
for the oppressed

**QUAKER
TESTIMONY AND
RACIAL JUSTICE**

TRUTH

We must witness that slavery,
colonialism and white
supremacy were and are wrong

COMMUNITY

How are we valuing all,
and ensuring all are
treated justly?

Justice

European culture and education systems do not explain, and often obfuscate, how European wealth was, "derived in no small part from the coffee and tobacco, cotton and diamonds, gold and sweat, and blood and death of the colonies".[94] Specific examples include the railways and canals in the Netherlands that were paid for with the proceeds of the coffee, sugar, indigo and plantations of Java in the Dutch East Indies.[95] The colonies were designed to extract resources for the metropole, with lasting implications for world infrastructure, meaning that in addition to the labour and deaths at the time, there is also a long term underdevelopment that will have a significant impact well into the future.

European powers have continued to benefit financially from the actions that they seek to distance themselves from. After the Haitian resistance won independence, France forced the new country into a debt of 81 million gold Francs under threat of re-invasion. The debt was for loss of property, perhaps meaning the land but also the enslaved people themselves. This debt was not paid in full until 1947 and even then by taking loans from French banks.[96] There is something deeply unjust about the idea that a European in the 20th century might receive the best healthcare available, partly as a result of government income from a debt forced upon people who were already victims of kidnapping and enslavement.

Continued privilege built upon colonial exploitation and enslavement is a moral injustice and firmly on the territory of faith groups. In 1986 British Quakers considered human rights at the primary gathering of what was then known as London Yearly Meeting. Part of the minute reads, "Above all we must take risks for God; look around us to the people who need help; listen to those who experience oppression; engage in the mutual process of liberation".[97] Everyone needs liberation because as Memmi argues that the colonial situations manufacture colonialists just as they manufacture the colonised.[98] The onus is therefore on white people to decolonise our lives, our organisations and our wealth.

Regardless of faith almost all white Europeans benefited from colonialism. We all have a responsibility to understand what proportion of our advantages come from this period, so that we can disempower ourselves from these benefits and seek to repair the harm caused.

Atonement

If Europe became wealthy through slavery and colonial domination it is not surprising that compensatory payments to the descendants of Africans who had been enslaved have been suggested. Reparations for slavery are "a means of restoring a community – in other words – a collective concern. Through individualism white culture encourages a self-centred human-over-nature point of view in which conquest and the accumulation of wealth are central preoccupations, consumption drives the economy, and 'us' verses 'them' thinking is the one form of community consciousness given support".[99]

Payments could be made from governments, corporations, religious institutions and other organisations that have benefited. Reparations could be direct payments, or equivalent funding for community or education projects where people of colour are the decision makers.

Quakers do not have a corporate position on reparations. This extended quote from the recent book *'What do Quakers believe?'* explains why this might be something that Quakers are ready to consider.

"If there were true equality in every aspect of life, the world would be transformed. It is a transformation that Quakers long for. Any inequality among people is offensive to them. They oppose all forms of hierarchy and do all they can to oppose it in their own affairs. Their whole religion and their entire way of life stem from their devotion to equality and their desire to give respect to all people. Society sees these as social issues, and they are political too, but for Quakers inequality is a religious matter. They regard it as a fundamental wickedness.

"One thing leads to another. No one changes overnight, but once people start thinking about equal rights their perceptions of the world begin to alter. They notice sink-holes in every path they tread: double standards of justice, double standards of truth, double standards everywhere." [100]

Appendices

Appendix A:
Additional milestones
in the story of colonialism
and the invention of race

The invention of race and the development of the transatlantic slave trade is not one story, but took place over hundreds of years and would be told differently by each of the tens of millions of people who were affected.

This timeline gives some starting points for further discovery. It includes important moments in the story of race and slavery that take place in Africa, the Americas and Europe, but it is not meant as a history of these continents. More than anything this section may leave you with a sense of more stories unheard, important history unknown.

1482 – A Portuguese ship sailed further south than any had done previously, landing in the Kingdom of the Kongo. This territory was 500 square kilometres and home to 2-3 million people. The people spoke KiKongo, traces of which are found in the Gullah dialect today spoken by some people living in coastal islands of Angola, Democratic Republic of Congo, and the US states of South Carolina and Georgia.[101] The Kingdom had existed since at least the 1300s and had a monarch (called the ManiKongo) chosen by an assembly of clan leaders. It had a form of forced labour, involving people captured in warfare, in debt, or judged to have broken the law.

1491 – Portugal set up a permanent representation in the capital, Mbanza Koongo (population 100,000). This was the first sustained encounter between a western European government and a sub-Saharan African government.[102] Portugal renamed Mbanza Koongo as São Salvador from 1568 to 1975. Mbanza Koongo is located in present day Angola, the country that 517 years after the Portuguese landed would bailout Portugal's economy following the 2008 financial crisis.[103]

1500 – A Portuguese expedition landed in Brazil, which would later receive millions of trafficked African people to work in mines and coffee plantations. Other European powers would use violence in the Caribbean to force African people to farm sugarcane.

1501 – European traffickers arrived with captive African people to Hispaniola, the first permanent settlement European settlement in the Americas (from the famous 'In 1492 Christopher Columbus sailed the ocean blue' story).

Thought to be known by indigenous people as Quizqueia, the island is now divided between two countries, Haiti and Dominican Republic.

1506 – A ManiKongo monarch called Nzinga Mbemba Afonso began his nearly 40 year reign and learned Portuguese. Afonso identified as Christian, following the conversion of his father, the previous ManiKongo.

Afonso was not against slavery and held some people in slavery himself. However he was opposed to the impact the European slave trade was having on his country. In a letter to the Portuguese King Joâo III in 1526 he wrote, "Each day the traders are kidnapping our people – children of this country, sons of our nobles and vassals, even people of our own family ... This corruption and depravity are so widespread that our land is entirely depopulated ... We need in this kingdom only priests and school teachers ... It is our wish that this kingdom not be a place for the trade or transport of slaves".

1530 – Five thousand people a year were trafficked through a port situated on the site where the Portuguese had landed almost 50 years earlier. Many people were bought from local headmen, chained together with their necks often in wooden yokes, and marched in large convoys to the coast. Often travelling in the dry season, they drank stagnant water and horrendous numbers of people died.[104]

By the end of the 1500s, fifteen thousand people per year were now being trafficked through the Kongo port. British,

French and Dutch ships also joined the slave trade, taking people from different locations on the west African coast. Slave ships started trafficking people on the longer journey to British colonies in North America.

1600s

The first European colonists of the Virginia colony have often been portrayed as fleeing religious persecution. A more significant motivation was greed and adding to their already considerable material wealth as members of the English elite. Tobacco production was highly profitable, but it required large areas of land and vast amounts of human labour.[105]

1610-1618 – Tenant farmers were shipped from England.

1619 – The first documented presence of African people in north America, brought by force aboard a Dutch ship. At first their treatment was less distinct from that of indentured servants from Europe than it would later become.

1630 – As the English elite sought to further increase profits, it was more common for labourers to be indentured servants, sent to work for 7 years before their release. The indenture system became increasingly exploitative. Conditions of this service where often ignored, and the lengths of service often extended.[106]

1640 – Three indentured servants were accused of running away from their owner together. When caught, they stood trial for the same offence. Each faced an immediate penalty of 30 lashes with a whip. A Dutchman named Victor and a Scotsman named James Gregory were then sentenced to four years additional service. However, an African man named John Punch was made a servant for life. The reason given for his harsher penalty was that he was 'a negro' - based on the Spanish term for the physical appearance of people of African descent.[107] This is the first recorded case of race being used to justify different servitude status.

1665 – The weakened army of the kingdom of the Kongo was defeated by the Portuguese army, and the ManiKongo was beheaded.[108]

Meanwhile in north America, it is after this point that people of European descent began to be defined as white. This was a decision by elite landowners in an attempt to counter unrest amongst labourers, such as the Bacon's Rebellion of 1696. Labourers of African and European descent were showing solidarity for each other, and implementing a racial hierarchy was an attempt to divide them.[i] Jeff Hitchcock describes this as a deal, in which "it was agreed that the elite of society could install slavery, provided that only Africans were enslaved".[109]

1680 – Enslavement of people of African descent began to be adopted within legal codes. The concept of white people and whiteness was established, in opposition to people of African descent and indigenous Americans. A

---

i. This was a very successful strategy with few exceptions. One was support for black resistance from Polish and some German workers in Haiti.

system of structural violence was established. The Virginia Slave Codes of 1705 are an example, introducing a law to prevent a white Christian labourer to be whipped naked, but legalised the murder of slaves by their 'master'. The law also explicitly banned the ownership of a white person by a black person and banned inter-racial marriage.[110] There is no record of a person of European descent being enslaved. The children of slaves were automatically considered property of the slave master, creating a structural incentive for women to have children, therefore causing them to be more likely to endure sexual violence by men.

History of slavery re-written to justify colonialism

1860s – Several European governments quickly forgot their slave trade history. For example, Britain only banned slavery in 1838) and within a few years they had begun to use combatting slavery as a stated motive for further colonial exploration. British and French criticisms of slavery at this time were not directed at Portugal and Spain that still allowed slavery in their colonies, but focused criticism on a, "distant, weak and safely non-white target" - the Arab controlled slave trade in East Africa.[111] In the same decade Europeans introduced breach-loading rifles and repeating rifles to their operations in Africa, weapons that shot further and more accurately then their predecessors.[112]

In the **mid-1870s**, whilst communities had been repeatedly decimated over centuries to feed the slave trade, eighty percent of the land area of Africa was under indigenous control. Exceptions were South Africa (Britain and the

Boers), Kingdom of the Kongo (Portugal) and some small islands and pockets of territory held by France and Spain.[113] The invention of race would now be used to take not just the people, but also the land.

1872 – When London's Albert Memorial was built in 1872 one of the statues was of a young black African, naked except leaves over his groin. The memorial's handbook explained that it was "representative of the uncivilised races" and that "broken chains at his feet refer to the part taken by Great Britain in the emancipation of the slaves".[114]

1870s – Celebrity travellers spread fictional accounts of journeys in Africa which were designed to appeal to newspaper editors by building on existing stereotypes and prejudices. The ultimate example was Henry Morton Stanley (not his real name of course which was John Rowlands, and he was not from the US, but from Denbigh in Wales). His life's work was to reinforce white supremacy, especially in the violence that he oversaw along the Nzadi/Nzere (Congo) river on behalf of his financial backers. His journalistic efforts spread a twisted view of people of colour with lines like, "For the half-castes I have great contempt".[115] He was knighted in 1899.

Reflection on the deep significance of this history today

The history of the white Christian church in slavery, colonialism and racism includes some horrific crimes and perverted religious defence and justifications as this quote from *King Leopold's Ghost* shows:

"Accordingly, with King Leopold's Ghost, *I was able to see more clearly not only how the colonial project's founding narrative was a story of power, greed, and plunder, but how such a story had come to be subsumed into the successor institution of the nation-state. It would be impossible to understand the current socio-political melodrama of the Congo, or any other African country for that matter, without drawing attention to this founding narrative".* [116]

"The founding story of the institutions of modern Africa rejects Africa itself. The story has shaped colonial Africa and continues to drive the successor institution, the nation-state ... Christianity uncritically assumes the same foundational narrative that denies and sacrifices Africa, and in the end becomes indistinguishable from the social sphere characterized by desperation, violence and corruption. In this way, Christianity not only lets down Africa; it also surrenders a key soteriological claim about Christ". [117]

— Emmanuel Katongole, Theologian (2011)

Appendix B:
European-level action on racism

European law and agreements about racism

Article 2 of the EU's principle document, the Treaty on European Union, declares the EU as founded on values that include human dignity and equality for all people, including people belonging to minorities.

For almost twenty years the European Union has had legislation that prohibits racial discrimination and requires member states to treat racist crime seriously, the Race Equality Directive (2000/43/EC), and the Framework Decision on racism and xenophobia (2008/913/JHA). The Race Equality Directive prohibits discrimination on the grounds of racial or ethnic origin in specific sectors. It covers both citizens and all others in the territory of an EU country. The Framework Decision on Combating Racism and Xenophobia penalises public incitement to violence and hatred on the basis of race, colour, religion, descent or national or ethnic origin.

Racial justice advocates can also make use of two other agreements. The Employment Equality Directive prohibits workplace discrimination on the basis of religion. The Audiovisual Media Services Directive bans incitement to hatred in audiovisual media services.

The EU Charter of Fundamental Rights became legally

binding in 2009. Article 21 prohibits discrimination on grounds that include, race, colour, ethnic origin, genetic features, language and religion.

The EU Fundamental Rights Agency (FRA) is an organisation offerring more hope. FRA is the source of research and public experience surveys on being Black in the EU, anti-Semitism and anti-Muslim hatred.

A less well known European body, the Council of Europe (covering a wider European area including non-EU countries such as Switzerland, Norway and Russia) provides the primary human rights framework for Europe. The Council of Europe's Protocol No. 12 is an extension to the European Convention of Human Rights that prohibits discrimination as a whole, rather than only in the application of one of the other convention rights.[118] Unfortunately, only 20 of the Council of Europe's 47 member states have ratified the protocol. Council of Europe member states are required to have anti-racism bodies, but many are poorly funded.

European-level projects

The EU budget has been used to support some anti-racism projects, of particular importance in countries where such support is not provided by national governments. This financial support includes:

- The Fundamental Rights and Citizenship Programme which seeks to reduce racism, xenophobia and anti-Semitism.

- The Programme for Employment and Social Solidarity (PROGRESS) provides some financial support to implement the principle of non-discrimination.

- The Europe for Citizens Programme provides support for remembrance projects.

These funding opportunities are small, but they do support activity that would otherwise not happen.

Other European projects have helped to spread ideas and practises relevant to anti-racism. The Council of Europe's Bologna Process is one example. The Bologna Process has contributed to developments in the French conversation on race by harmonising some elements of European higher education. This resulted in English language material on post-colonial approaches being brought to French university libraries. It was a helpful boost to the ideas of Ahmed Boubeker, Pap Ndiaye and other academics of colour.[119]

The human rights standards developed in Europe since the Holocaust have helped to ensure that peace and human dignity have been increasingly enjoyed in Europe over the last 70 years.[120]

Quaker research on hate speech and hate crime in Europe

Hate crime is crime that is motivated by hatred of a characteristic that the targeted person or people are perceived to hold. The QCEA report *'Hate Crime:*

Prevention and Restoration in the EU' (2015) provides a detailed examination of hate crime in Europe. In particular, we noted the substantial under-reporting of hate crime and made recommendations to improve community justice processes and give victims more confidence to report hate crime.[121]

In 2018 QCEA published a study on violent and dehumanising hate speech against migrants and refugees. The report, *Anti-Migrant Hate Speech*,[122] provided new information about the extent of hate speech on the website comment sections of some of Europe's biggest selling newspapers. Our research identified the successful counter-hate speech initiatives that QCEA believe could be used throughout Europe, should the necessary financial support be provided.

References and notes

1. QCEA has worked to reduce anti-migrant political discourse and racism since the 1980s. Direct migrant work in our early years led to engagment with the European Commission, World Council of Churches and others in 1989. Work intensified in the early 1990s with QCEA leading working groups on anti-racism legislation in Brussels, including moderating the Churches Commission for Migrants in Europe (CCME) working group on racism, a large racism conference, and drafting a Council of Europe resolution on the rise of neo-fascism. Publications included: *Strangers in a Foreign Land* (1991) and *Between Hope and Disaster: Aspects of Neo-Fascism in Europe* (1993). In the late 1990s QCEA successfully lobbied MEPs on vote to set up the Monitoring Centre for Racism and Xenophobia, co-founded the European Network against Racism, and advocated for Article 13 of the Amsterdam Treaty on proactive promotion of non-discrimination of race, gender, age, disability, and sexual orientation.

2. Research into attitudes of white Remain supporters in Britain found that they present Britain as newly xenophobic and insular. Katie Wright Higgins (2018) found that the privilege of white respondents led them to overlook the racial exclusion at the core of British society. See: Higgins, Katie Wright (2018) *'National Belonging Post-Referendum: Britons Living in other EU Member States Respond to Brexit'* in Benson, Michaela and Lewis, Chantelle (2019), *Brexit, British People of Colour in the EU-27 and everyday racism in Britain and Europe*. Ethnic and Racial Studies, ISSN 0141-9870 [Available online: *http://research.gold. ac.uk/26060/*]

3. DiAngelo, R. (2016) *What Does it Mean to be White? Developing White Racial Literacy*, Revised Edition. Peter Lang: New York p101.

4. ibid., p98.

5. ibid.

6. Harvey, J (2014) *Dear White Christians: For Those Still Longing for Racial Reconciliation* (Grand Rapids, MI) p45.

7. DiAngelo, op. cit., p130.

8. Tochluk, S. (2016). *Living in the Tension: The quest for a spiritualised racial justice*, pp117-118.

9. *Quakers and race* (unknown issue from about 1994), reprinted in *Rediscovering our Social Testimony (ROST) responses and challenges*, in Jonathan Dale and others (2000) *Faith in Action: Quaker social testimony*. Quaker Books: London.

10. DiAngelo, op. cit., p134.

11. ibid., p109.

12. ibid., p46.

13. *The Guardian* (4 December 2018) 'Revealed: the stark evidence of everyday racial bias in Britain'. Available at: *https://www.theguardian.com/uk-news/2018/dec/02/revealed-the-stark-evidence-of-everyday-racial-bias-in-britain*

14. DiAngelo, op. cit., p193-4.

15. Silverstein, P. (2018) *Postcolonial France Race, Islam, and the Future of the Republic: Urban marginalisation, police violence and institutional discrimination in modern France*. Pluto: New York, p84.

16. Ethnic and religious minorities represent at least 7 percent of the EU population. In the UK, 8.5 million people (13.5% of the population) are people of colour. France does not produce population statistics by race, but it is estimated France includes 3.5 million Muslims, 97% of which are people of colour. See: Fernandez, C. 'EU institutions failing race equality drive'. 5 September 2016. Available online at: *https://www.euractiv.com/section/future-eu/opinion/diversity-in-the-eu-institutions-how-the-eu-bubble-has-failed-race-equality/*

17. DiAngelo, op. cit., p107.

18. Research is increasingly being undertaken into implicit / unconscious bias. This is the idea that people may disfavour somone based on social group membership, but without the intention to do so. For example, whilst looking for accommodation for a holiday a White person might have an implicit bias in favour of a B&B owner/ host with a White sounding name. The way to address implicit biases is to understand them, so we can begin to interrupt them.

19. Akala (Daley, K) 2018, *Natives: Race and class in the ruins of empire*. Two Roads: London p53.

20. Harvey, op.cit., p12.

21. Tochluk, op. cit., p99.

22. Benson, Michaela and Lewis, Chantelle (2019). 'Brexit, British People of Colour in the EU-27 and everyday racism in Britain and Europe'. *Ethnic and Racial Studies*, ISSN 0141-9870 [Available online: *http:// research.gold.ac.uk/26060/*] p11.

23. Crisp, J. 'Is the European Union too White?' 26 August 2016. Available online at: *https://www.euractiv.com/section/future-eu/ video/is-the-european-commission-too-white/*

24. *European Commission* (2017) 'Communication of the Commission - A better workplace for all: from equal opportunities towards diversity and inclusion' - C(2017) 5300. Available online at: *https://ec.europa. eu/info/sites/info/files/communication-equal-opportunities-diversity- inclusion-2017.pdf*

25. Quoted in Durham, G (2018) *What do Quakers believe?* Quaker Quicks / Christian Alternative: Winchester, pp-27-8..

26. DiAngelo, op. cit., p131.

27. ibid., p134.

28. Akala, op.cit., p39.

29. Doll Test – Italy: *https://youtu.be/QRZPw-9sJtQ*

30. The dominant view is that Roman and Greek thought included cultural rather than racial distinction and discrimination, but there are some descenting voices. Mudimbe, Y.V. (1988) *The Invention of Africa: Gnosis, Philosophy and the Order of Knowledge*. Indiana University Press, p88.

31. Others argue that the development of racial politics can be seen in the construction of the Spanish identity in the 1500s (as a White and Catholic space), developed in opposition to both communities expelled from Spain and people encountered during Spanish colonial exploration in the Americas. See: Vives, L (2010) 'White Europe: an alternative reading of the Southern EU border'. *Journal of Geopolitica(s)*, 2011, vol. 2. p58.

32. Vives, L (2010) 'White Europe: an alternative reading of the Southern EU border'. *Journal of Geopolitica(s)*, 2011, vol. 2. p53.

33. About 1.6 million people were trafficked to the British-controlled Caribbean and 400 thousand people to British colonies in North America. French and Dutch colonies in the Caribbean received 1.6 million and 500 thousand trafficked people, respectively. More than 3.6 million people were trafficked to Portuguese controlled land, and 1.5 million to Spanish controlled land in South America. A major, but more protracted source of misery and death was the spread of virulent diseases by colonial Europeans.

34. Akala, op. cit., p140.

35. Hitchcock, J (2008) 'Quakers and Reparations for Slavery and Jim Crow'. Article, 11 October 2008 available at: *www.reparationsthecure.org*

36. ibid.

37. Africa Museum website, history section. See: *https://www.africamuseum.be/en/discover/history*. Accessed February 2019.

38. Hoffman, P. (2015). *Why Did Europe Conquer the World?* Princeton University Press. p2.

39. Mudimbe, Y.V. (1988) *The Invention of Africa: Gnosis, Philosophy and the Order of Knowledge*. Indiana University Press, p30. The relevance of the gender of dominant philosophers is also apparent in this quote, and other references to virgin areas needing to be penetrated.

40. Akala, op. cit., p3.

41. See: (1) *BBC NEWS Online* (2013) 'Mau Mau torture victims to receive compensation'. *https://www.bbc.com/news/uk-22790037* – and (2) Akala, op. cit., p145.

42. Harvey, op. cit., p52.

43. 'Black Pete' is a character created for a story book written in 1850 by Amsterdam school teacher Jan Schenkman. The character is a central part of public celebrations on 5 and 6 December. He is portrayed using colonial stereotypes, such as big red lips and gold earrings, and most significantly he is played by white performers using make up to present a 'blackface' caricature of black people that gained popularity during the 19th century and contributed to the spread of racial stereotypes.

44. Akala, op. cit., p5.

45. Jeater, D (2018) *Bearing witness or bearing whiteness? The 2018 Salter Lecture at the Britain Yearly Meeting*. Available at *https://www.youtube.com/watch?v=z5cpQofRubU*

46. *European Network Against Racism (ENAR)* 2016. 'Racism and Discrimination in the Context of Migration in Europe. ENAR Shadow Report 2015-16'. pp10-11. Available online at: *http://www.enar-eu.org/IMG/pdf/shadowreport_2015x2016_long_low_res.pdf*

47. Silverstein, op. cit., p46.

48. For some context, see for example: *https://www.theguardian.com/media/2018/dec/11/the-sun-newspaper-reporting-sterling-race*

49. Silverstein, op. cit., pp 11, 45.

50. United Nations Group of Experts on People of African Decent, Statement to the media on the conclusion of its official visit to Belgium, 4-11 February 2019.

51. Silverstein, op. cit., p43.

52. ibid., p14.

53. ibid., p59.

54. ibid., p16.

55. See his Washington Post article at: *https://www.washingtonpost.com/news/global-opinions/wp/2016/11/03/obsessing-over-europes-refugee-crisis-while-ignoring-africas-is-white-privilege-at-work/?utm_term=.c4433e015d0a*

56. *QCEA (2017) 'Child Immigration Detention in Europe'. http://www.qcea.org/wp-content/uploads/2017/07/Child-immigration-detention-in-Europe.pdf*

57. In 2016, QCEA staff met with Ambassadors and other officials that sit on the relevant EU decision-making committee to discuss the protection of human rights and encouraged a larger civilian maritime presence to help save lives at sea. Our engagement has continued with EU, NATO and Italian parliamentarians.

58. For more information, visit: *www.QCEA.org/mff*

59. Goldberg, David Theo (2006) 'Racial Europeanization' in Benson, Michaela and Lewis, Chantelle (2019). *Brexit, British People of Colour in the EU-27 and everyday racism in Britain and Europe*. Ethnic and Racial Studies, ISSN 0141-9870 [Available online: *http://research.gold.ac.uk/26060/*] p5.

60. In particular, European governments can be encouraged and held to account for their compliance with the European Charter of Fundamental Rights (the 28 EU members only) and European Convention on Human Rights (all 48 European states except Belarus). These international agreements are at risk of being watered down.

61. In general, the data available on hate crime in Europe is of low and inconsistent quality. Each year, several European countries do not report any hate crime having taken place at all. In 2016, a new process began that expects to develop a common methodology to record and collect hate crime data, known as the High Level Group on combating Racism, Xenophobia and other forms of Intolerance. It

brings together different EU institutions, with the Council of Europe, Organisation for Security and Cooperation in Europe and United Nations High Commissioner for Refugees.

62. Jeater, op. cit.

63. Silverstein, op. cit., p13.

64. Quoted in Dower, N. (ed) (2008). *Nonsense on Stilts? A Quaker view of Human Rights*. Ebor Press, York. p19.

65. European Network Against Racism (ENAR), op. cit.

66. Akala, op. cit., p304.

67. European Network Against Racism (ENAR), op. cit., p10.

68. *Euractiv*. 'Hungarian official admits campaign to generate hate against migrants'. 7 September 2015. Available at: *http://www.euractiv.com/section/justice-home-affairs/news/hungarian-official-admits-campaign-to-generate-hate-against-migrants/*

69. After the Second World War and the Holocaust, European countries signed the European Convention on Human Rights, and established the Council of Europe to oversee the protection of human rights and democracy in Europe. Completely separate from the European Union, it now includes every country in Europe except Belarus.

70. *Council of Europe* (2016) 'Annual Report on ECRI's Activities'. Available online at: *http://www.coe.int/t/dghl/monitoring/ecri/activities/Annual_Reports/Annual%20report%202016.pdf*

71. Emejulu, A. (2017) *On the hideous whiteness of Brexit*. Available online at: *https://www.versobooks.com/blogs/2733-on-the-hideous-whiteness-of-brexit-let-us-be-honest-about-our-past-and-our-present-if-we-truly-seek-to-dismantle-white-supremacy*

72. Benson, Michaela and Lewis, Chantelle (2019). 'Brexit, British People of Colour in the EU-27 and everyday racism in Britain and Europe'. Ethnic and Racial Studies, ISSN 0141-9870 [Available online: *http://research.gold.ac.uk/26060/*] p9.

73. Silverstein, op. cit., p57.

74. Akala, op. cit., p305.

75. Quakers in Britain, (2018) *Owning Power and Privilege: Toolkit for Action*. Quaker Peace and Social Witness, p15.

76. Tochluk, op. cit., p177.

77. Quote from Adam Hochschild's *King Leopold's Ghost* p135, in Katongole, Emmanuel (2011) *The Sacrifice of Africa: A Political Theology for Africa*: Eerdman: Cambridge, p18.

78. DiAngelo, op. cit., p134.

79. Talk by Jamie Bartlett to Full Circle discussion group in Brussels, 6 June 2017.

80. Julye, Vanessa (2019) 'Are we ready to make the necessary changes?' *Friends Journal*, themed issue looking at 'A Racially Diverse Society of Friends?' January 2019. (Philadelphia: Available online at: *www.FriendsJourmal.org*).

81. Hitchcock, op. cit.

82. Harvey, op. cit., p200.

83. ibid., p203.

84. ibid., pp 199-200.

85. ibid., pp 207-8.

86. Ela, Jean-Marc. In Katongole, Emmanuel (2011) *The Sacrifice of Africa: A Political Theology for Africa:* Eerdman: Cambridge, p22.

87. Gerbner, K (2018) *Christian Slavery: Conversion and Race in the Protestant Atlantic World*. University of Pennsylvania Press: Philadelphia. pp 48-73.

88. ibid., p58.

89. In north America people of colour were not admitted into membership of the Religious Society of Friends until the 1780s, and even then in small numbers and with more difficult procedures. See: Julye, Vanessa (2019) 'Are we ready to make the necessary changes?' *Friends Journal*, themed issue looking at 'A Racially

Diverse Society of Friends?' January 2019. (Philadelphia: Available online at: *www.FriendsJourmal.org*)

90. Hitchcock, op. cit.

91. Julye, op. cit., p11.

92. *Soul Work: Antiracist Theologies in Dialogue*, edited by Marjorie Bowens-Wheatley and Nancy Palmer Jones, 171-198. Boston: Skinner House, 2003.

93. Michael Bartlet in Dower, N. (ed) (2008). *Nonsense on Stilts? A Quaker view of Human Rights*. Ebor Press, York. P17.

94. Akala, op. cit., pp6-7.

95. Hochschild, A (1998) *King Leopold's Ghost: A Story of Greed, Terror and Heroism in Colonial Africa*. New York: Mariner Books, p37

96. Akala, op. cit., p131.

97. Dower, N. (ed) (2008). Nonsense on Stilts? A Quaker view of Human Rights. Ebor Press, York. p98

98. Silverstein, op. cit., p14.

99. Hitchcock, op. cit.

100. Durham, G (2018) *Quaker Quicks - What Do Quakers Believe? Everything you always wanted to know about Quakerism*. John Hunt Publishing: London.

101. Hochschild, op. cit., pp 8-11.

102. ibid., p8.

103. Jeater, op. cit.
104. Hochschild, op. cit., p10

105. Harvey, op. cit., p48.

106. ibid.

107. ibid., p50.

108. Hochschild, op. cit., p15

109. Hitchcock, op. cit.

110. Akala, op.cit., p131.

111. Hochschild, op. cit., p27-28.

112. ibid., p89.

113. ibid., p42.

114. ibid., p28.

115. ibid., p30. See also Speke in central Africa.

116. Katongole, Emmanuel (2011) *The Sacrifice of Africa: A Political Theology for Africa*: Eerdman: Cambridge, p16.

117. ibid., p21.

118. Council of Europe, op. cit.

119. Silverstein, op. cit., p6.

120. European governments have also been working together to develop capacity for supporting peacebuilding in recent years, and have relevant experience that could be used to more effectively to address the root causes of forced migration. Examples include, the EU's unarmed confidence building mission in Georgia, and funding for non-governmental peacebuilding organisations to work in violent conflicts in many parts of the world.

121. *QCEA* (2015) 'Hate Crime: Prevention and Restoration in the EU'. Available online at: *http://www.qcea.org/wp-content/uploads/2015/05/Hate-Crime-Background-Paper-final.sla_.pdf*

122. Available online at: *https://www.qcea.org/2018/06/anti-migrant-hate-speech-report-published/*